Genjokoan

by

Zen Master Dogen

With commentary by

Albert Low

Introduction

Dogen's Genjokoan is undoubtedly a very difficult text. It is difficult in the same way that the koans of the Mumonkan are difficult. Reading and working with the Genjokoan is a form of zazen and reading it requires the same kind of devoted attention as does zazen.

When reading the following, it is best to begin by reading Dogen's Genjokoan several times before reading my commentaries on it. As I explain later I have used a number of translations as a basis for Dogen's poem, and you might like to read these other versions (www.thezensite.com) before going on to my meditations. Try to read the Genjokoan as a form of prolonged zazen. Moreover, rather than reading it as though it were a kind of philosophical text, try to read it as you would a poem. Just as a poem, if you read it a number of times, becomes ever more rich, so reading Dogen's *Genjokoan* will become richer by repeated readings.

Zazen is often translated as 'meditation,' but this is not quite right. Zazen includes meditation, but it also includes 'concentration' and 'contemplation.' These are not different activities of the mind, but are different emphases in the direction the mind takes when seeking to transcend experience. I understand meditation to mean 'to take an idea, a phrase, or a statement, and allow the mind to *dwell* on it.'

I deliberately used the word 'dwell,' but I could equally well have used 'inhabit' or 'reside.' These are living words evoking the sense of 'home,' particularly in the sense that Hakuin used the word in his *Chant in Praise of Zazen*, "Coming and going we never leave home."

1

'To dwell' on an idea is quite the opposite of 'to think about' it. Although, originally, to meditate meant 'to think over,' 'reflect,' or 'consider,' it came to be used in a religious context and acquired quite a different meaning. When we think about an idea we try to break it down into its constituent parts, that is to say we analyze it. We then try to combine these parts with other parts of ideas that have been similarly analyzed, and so reach a new synthesis or understanding. When we meditate, we do not *seek* greater understanding. We seek to *allow* understanding to come home to us. This often comes as an insight. We can only meditate on live ideas. A live idea is one that is not arrived at by thinking, but through insight.

In the West, we have, for the most part, lost sight of the transcendent. We now believe that experience alone can show us the way to truth, and we believe that reason is the means by which we can refine experience into theories. However, experience can only show us the surface, the appearance; it cannot penetrate to the reality that underlies the appearance. Meditation, as I am using the word, is the gateway that leads beyond the surface to the transcendent. Meditation, therefore, leaves the surface and penetrates ever deeper into the depths. The deeper the penetration, the more alive the idea that emerges. This is why it is important, when you are meditating, to meditate on the words of an awakened person; the deeper the awakening that he or she has attained, the richer your meditation will be.

To concentrate is to hold the mind steady on a center or focal point. The most frequently used concentration practice is mantra practice. Most of the time our mind is filled with random thoughts and images and is essentially unstable. Concentration on a mantra brings some order into the mind. Stability and order are essential qualities when reading the Genjokoan.

Contemplation originally meant, "to gaze attentively, to observe." To gaze implies to observe steadily, unwaveringly. In its religious context it also implies to gaze with wonder or awe. At its deepest level, contemplation would be to stand in the presence of God, ultimately to be one with God, or with the transcendent.

As I said at the beginning of this introduction, contemplation, concentration, and meditation, are not separate and distinct activities of mind: it is a question of emphasis. All three will be involved to some degree when pondering the Genjokoan.

A way to deepen your pondering is to write down what comes to you. This is a form of what Hakuin called "verbal prajna." With verbal prajna, meditation comes to the fore. By writing down what we arrive at through meditation, we introduce a new discipline into the process. Writing requires clarity, simplicity and completeness. In zazen, the main value of meditation is not so much to arrive at a new understanding, but to break up one's adherence to old understanding. It prepares the way to allow contemplation to come to the fore. Concentration steadies the mind and so allows contemplation to be possible.

In the practice of zazen, flexibility of mind is essential. This is why we are exhorted to let go of all goals and reasons for practice. These simply fix the mind. One of the main hindrances to the practice of zazen is the belief that we have to concentrate in order to get an answer to a problem, or to achieve a particular state of mind.

THE VERSES OF THE GENJOKOAN

1) Seeing that all things are the Buddha dharma, there is awakening, illusion, practice, life, death, buddhas and sentient beings.

2) Seeing all things do not exist there is no illusion, no realization, no buddha, no sentient being, no birth and death.

3) Since the Buddha way is beyond form and emptiness, there are birth and death, delusion and enlightenment, sentient beings and buddhas.

4) Yet, while this is true, and in spite of our wish that it were otherwise, flowers fall, and weeds spring up, even though we do not want them to.

5) Reaching out to experience the world is illusion; to allow the world to come to you is awakening. To awaken to the dream is buddhahood; to dream about awakening is to be an ordinary person.

6) Moreover, some even awaken after awakening, and others dream about the dream. An awakened person does not know he is awakened. Yet, even so, an awakened person continues to be an awakened person.

7) Perceiving forms and sounds with a unified mind is intimate perception, unlike reflections in a mirror or the moon reflected on water: when one side is light and the other is darkness.

8) To know the Buddha Way is to know the self; to know the self is to forget the self; to forget the self is to be one with the ten thousand things. To be one with the ten thousand things means body and mind of oneself and others drop away. No trace of awakening remains, and traceless awakening goes on without end. At first, to seek the dharma is to be separate from the dharma. With authentic transmission true self is revealed.

9) When sailing in a boat, and looking just towards the riverbank, one has the illusion that the shore is moving. But by fixing one's gaze just on the boat, one will see that the boat is moving. Similarly, viewing the ten thousand things with a confused mind we mistakenly believe that the mind and things are permanent. But, with the clarity of practice we will see that mind and things are empty.

10) Firewood turns to ash and cannot return to being firewood, but we should not believe that ash comes after and firewood before. Firewood is firewood and, having its past and future, is still independent of past and future. Ash is ash and has its own past and future. Just as firewood does not return to being firewood after it has become ash, we do not return to birth after death. This is the established rule of Buddhism, and birth is known as the unborn. It is also the established rule of Buddhism that death does not become life. Thus death is known as no-death. Birth is now; death is now: just like winter and spring. We do not believe that winter becomes spring, nor spring, summer.

11) Coming to awakening is like the moon being reflected on water: the moon does not get wet nor is the water disturbed. Even though the moon's light is extensive, it can be reflected in the shallowest of puddles. The great moon and the whole sky are reflected in a single drop of water. Awakening does not affect you any more than the moon disturbs the water. You cannot obstruct awakening just as a puddle cannot obstruct the moonlight. The depth of the puddle is conditional on the height of the moon.

12. When awakening is still mentally and physically incomplete, we believe that we have arrived. But with full awakening we feel something is missing. For example, if you sail to the middle of the ocean with no land in sight and look around in the four directions, the ocean looks circular with no distinguishing features. But the ocean is neither round nor square and its features are infinite. To fish, it is like a palace; to the gods it is like a jewelled necklace. But, as far as we are concerned, it is simply a vast circle of water. Though the material world and the transcendent world have a variety of features, you see and understand only what your eye of practice allows you to reach. So, if we want to know the way things really are, we should be aware that the oceans and mountains have an infinite number of aspects other than appearing square or round. We should also remember that there are other worlds in the four directions, not only out in space but also right here and now even in a drop of water.

13. A fish swims in the ocean, and regardless of how far it goes it does not come to the end of the water. A bird flies in the sky, and regardless of how far it flies it does not come to the end of the sky. However, the fish does not leave the water nor does the bird leave the sky. It is just that when they need to go far the sky and ocean are large; when they do not need to go far, the ocean and sky are small.

In this way, each fulfills itself to the utmost and uses its element to the fullest extent. If a bird should leave the sky it would instantly die and a fish would instantly die if it left the water. Water is life, the air is life; the fish is life, the bird is life. Many variations on this idea are possible: there is practice and awakening; there are people and activity.

14. But if a bird tries to fly beyond the sky, or if a fish tries to swim beyond the ocean they will have no way to do so, nor will there be any beyond. If we find the Way our daily activities manifest awakening; all our actions are the supreme reality. This Way is neither large nor small, self nor other, it does not exist from before, nor does it appear for the first time now, it is just thus.

15. Therefore, when practicing the Buddha Way, when realizing one aspect one thoroughly penetrates that aspect; when engaged in one activity one is fully engaged in that activity. Now is the place; Now the way unfolds, We cannot know the limits of what can be known because this knowledge comes at the same time as awakening. Do not think that

what you have seen into will inevitably be known consciously and will be recognized by your intellect. Although one awakens to the inconceivable all at once, it will not be experienced. How can it be?

16. Zen master Pao-ch'e of Mount Ma-ku was fanning himself. A monk came and asked, "Wind, by its very nature, just keeps blowing, and there is nowhere it cannot reach. Why then do you need to use a fan?" The master replied, "You only know that the nature of wind is to keep blowing; you do not yet know the true meaning of 'there is nowhere it cannot reach.'" The monk then asked, "What is the true meaning of 'there is nowhere it does not reach'?" The master just fanned himself. The monk bowed deeply.

This is like authentic practice. Someone who says that because the wind just keeps blowing we do not need to use a fan, or even, even if we do not use [a fan] we can still feel the wind blowing, does not know ever-presence, and does not know ' there is nowhere it does not reach.' Because the very nature of wind is to keep blowing. The Buddha's Way reveals the Earth to be pure gold, and the Milky Way the sweetest of creams.

MEDITATIONS ON THE GENJOKOAN

"IT HAS NO FORM YET IT APPEARS"

"You should energetically discipline yourself to get at the meaning itself. The meaning alone is with itself and leads to Nirvana. Words are bound up with discrimination and lead to rebirth. Meaning is attained from much learning, and this much learning means to be conversant with meanings and not with words. To be conversant with meaning means to ascertain the view which is not at all associated with any philosophical school, and which will keep not only yourself but others as well from falling into false views. Let seekers for meaning reverently approach those who are much learned in it, but those who are attached to words as being in accord with meaning, they are to be left to themselves and to be shunned by truth seekers."

    The Lankavatara Sutra[1]

I would like to write something on the Genjokoan. I should like to do so both for others and for myself in the hope that we all may enter more deeply into the mystery of being. If I write for myself there is a chance that I shall be honest; if I write for others I will have to be as clear and simple as possible. To write honestly is to write from one's own understanding and not to copy the style or content of others. Parroting the words and style of others, and pretending they are one's own, seems to be an occupational hazard among Zen Buddhist authors.

Yet here I encounter my first difficulty, and it is one that in the eyes of many will disqualify me from having anything worthwhile to say about the Genjokoan. I do not speak

---

[1] Suzuki D.T. 1978 *The Lankavatara Sutra* Tr. D.T. (Boulder: Prajna Press) p. 169

Japanese, not even modern Japanese, let alone 13th century Japanese. The 13th century was when Dogen lived and wrote his masterpiece. Because I do not speak or understand Japanese, I will have to rely on the translations of others, but will this not mean that right from the beginning I will be using others' words?

The difficulty is made worse because numerous translations are available, and none of them agree with one another. The zensite website (www.thezensite.com) gives a compilation of seven translations.[2] These do not always agree with one another about many of the important points that Dogen is making; furthermore they sometimes contradict each other. How can someone, who does not speak Japanese, decide which among these is a reliable translation that would be useful as a basis for a commentary?

A last difficulty is perhaps the most serious. Not only do I not speak Japanese, I also live in a culture very far removed from the culture in which Dogen lived. I live in a culture that has its roots deeply in the Christian-Judaic traditions. It is also a culture that has passed through "the Age of Reason," and so is a

---

[2] Translators

Robert Aitken and Kazuaki Tanahashi. Revised at San Francisco Zen Center, and later at Berkeley Zen Center; published (2000) in Tanahashi, *Enlightenment Unfolds* (Boston: Shambhala).

Norman Waddell and Masao Abe (2002), in *The Heart of Dōgen's Shōbōgenzō* (Albany: SUNY Press), 39-45.

Paul Jaffe (1996), in Yasutani, *Flowers Fall* (Boston: Shambhala), 101-107.

Gudo Wafu Nishijima, from "*Understanding the Shōbōgenzō*", © Windbell Publications.

Francis H. Cook (1989), in *Sounds of Valley Streams* (Albany: SUNY Press), 65-9.

Thomas Cleary (1986), published 2005 in *Classics of Buddhism and Zen* V.2 (Boston: Shambhala), 275-80.

Kosen Nishiyama and John Stevens (1975) (www.thezensite.com)

Reiho Masunaga (www.thezensite.com)

culture where reason and intellectual activity predominate. In our culture we tend to live in the world as observers rather than participants. Dogen lived in a culture that was based on the Shinto/Buddhist tradition, and in which Zen Buddhism was beginning to exert its influence; it had not heard of "the Age of Reason." This culture was primarily a farming culture in which participation in the cycle of the seasons was paramount. Does this not further exclude me from having anything worthwhile to say about Dogen's Genjokoan?

However, all is not lost. I must emphasize that I am not trying to explain Dogen's text, or put it into different words. I am not saying, "This is what Dogen really means." Similarly, when working on a koan, I do not try to explain it or try to find more appropriate words for it. The Genjokoan is what it says it is: a koan. To work on a koan we do not start with the words, and then struggle to understand what they mean, as we do, for example, when reading a philosophical text. A basic koan is, "What is your face before your parents were born?" The only way to work with this koan is *to be* your face before your parents were born, and then to see how the koan expresses this face. Moreover, this face does not differ according to the fashions and ways of thinking of a culture.

Let me repeat the words from the Lankavatara sutra that I used as the epigraph to this essay: *To be conversant with meaning means to ascertain the view which is not at all associated with any philosophical school, and which will keep not only yourself but others as well from falling into false views.* "The view which is not at all associated with any philosophical school" will also be a universal view that is not tainted by cultural values and beliefs. 'Meaning' moreover obviously does not mean the dictionary meaning. Nor does it mean 'meaning' as derived from context.

The word 'tree' has multiple meanings depending on the context in which the word is used. For example, 'tree' in the context of a forest has a different meaning to the meaning of 'tree' in the context of Christmas (Christmas tree), or the family tree, or the Tree of Life. 'Your face before your parents were born' has no context. This means that from the point of view of 'contextual meaning' the words have no meaning. For this reason many people consider the koans of Zen to be obscure, illogical and meaningless.

As the koan has no contextual meaning, the question, "What is your face before your parents were born?" has no answer, where an 'answer' would be a clarification of the context. The normal answer to the question, "What is a tree?" is, "It grows in a forest, has branches and leaves...." Or, "It appears at the beginning of the family bible and has the names, birth-dates and deaths of the different generations of the family."

So how do I answer the question, "What is you face before your parents were born?"? The only way, let me repeat, is to *be the face*. This is also the way to work on the Genjokoan. The words of the Genjokoan, as well as the words of the koans and mondo, are not descriptive or explanatory words; they are *evocative* words. They do not, moreover, evoke feelings, thoughts or images; they evoke 'the truth,' or 'Buddha nature.' For example, "A monk asked Joshu, 'What is Buddha?' Joshu replied, 'The oak tree in the garden.'

Hakuin said that to work on Zen we need Great Faith, Great Doubt and Great Perseverance. Great Faith is not Great Faith in anything particular such as Buddha, Buddhist teaching, or Buddhist practice. Faith is not the same as belief. Knowing is our true home and faith is knowing in action. To work on a koan, we allow our 'knowing' to act freely without the support of knowledge or understanding and without the impediment of having to conform to logical structures, other people's ideas, or traditional teaching. This is Great Faith.

The psychologist C.G. Jung stayed with the words of the koans and concluded that they "not only border on the grotesque but are right there in the middle of it, and sound like the most crashing nonsense."[3] Alas, the translators of the Genjokoan that I have cited seemed to have stayed with the words and were primarily concerned with producing a correct, literal translation of the Genjokoan, and, sometimes, wrote the 'most crashing nonsense.'

Although koans do not conform to logical structures, they are not "the most crashing nonsense," and Dogen's Genjokoan makes perfect sense, as we shall see in what follows, even though much of it is, at first glance, extremely obscure. Dogen was a deeply awakened man and he was writing from that awakened state. The Genjokoan is a 'description' or evocation of the awakened state. To work with him, we must work from our own awakened state.

I have read some commentators who say that koans can be resolved in any number of ways. They seemed to have looked upon koans as something like verbal Rorschach tests, in which one is encouraged to allow the mind to flow as freely as possible. This, however, is not so. There is only one acceptable response to any koan. That is a response from, and expressing, 'Buddha nature.' For example, the only acceptable response to the question "Who are you?" is you.

---

[3] Jung C.G.(1958) Psychology and Religion Translated by R.F.C.Hull (Routledge and Kegan Paul: London.) p. 539.

But, perhaps I should say something more about Dogen before going further. You can read what I have to say in any book about Dogen or, if you prefer, on the web. But I may save you some time.

He was born in 1200 as a member of the powerful Murakami branch of the Genji clan. He was two years old when his father died, and eight years old when his mother died. He entered the Buddhist priesthood at the age of 13, and soon was struggling with a life koan: if, as is widely taught in Buddhism, all beings are Buddha, why do we have to work so hard to awaken to this truth? He met a Japanese Rinzai teacher, Esai, and worked with koan practice for several years, but became disenchanted with this. Later he became the student of Myozen, a former disciple of Esai. Together, Myozen and Dogen went to China in order to go deeper into the practice of Zen.

Just before they were scheduled to leave, Myozen's teacher Myoyu became seriously ill. Myozen called all of the disciples together and asked them whether he should continue with his plans to go to China, or whether he should stay in Japan and look after his teacher. All of them, including Dogen, counselled him to put off the trip. However, Myozen said,

"Even if I were to stay, it would not prolong the life of this dying man. Even if I took care of him, I could not put an end to his suffering. Even if I were to comfort him on his deathbed, I could do nothing to help him escape from the cycle of birth and death. All of this would be of no use whatsoever in my renunciation of the world and attainment of the Way, and might even lead to evil acts by interfering with my determination to seek the dharma. However, if I proceed with my determination to visit China and attain even a small measure of enlightenment it will benefit many people ...To waste valuable time for the sake of just one person is not the way of Buddhism."

After he had arrived in China, Dogen met a Chinese master, Nyojo. Nyojo was a strict disciplinarian, and, out of compassion, goaded his students on by striking, with his fist or a slipper, those who fell asleep in the zendo. He told Dogen to cut off completely all attachments and to immerse himself in his practice. He said that the mind must be soft and fluid, abiding nowhere. One night the monk sitting next to Dogen fell asleep, and in a loud voice the master yelled, "Zazen is to drop off body and mind! Why are you sleeping?" When he heard this Dogen was deeply awakened.

To be awakened is to perceive and live in a new way. Although awakening is often accompanied by an emotion or experience, awakening is not simply an experience. One of the mistakes that people make when practicing Zen is to look for a special experience: an experience of space, of a heightened emotion, of some kind of vision or new understanding. To say awakening is to perceive and live in a new way is not quite right and it might be better to say that awakening is to live naturally; it is a 'new way' because most of us live very unnatural lives.

Zen Master Echo, in a verse he added to koan number 40 of the Hekinganroku, wrote of the awakened state in this way:

> Hearing, seeing, touching, and knowing are not one and one;
> Mountains and rivers are not to be seen in a mirror.
> The frosty sky, the setting moon - at midnight;
> With whom will the serene waters of the lake reflect the shadows in the cold?

What does the word 'Genjokoan' mean?

Yasutani tells us that the Japanese word *genjo* means 'all phenomena, the whole universe, the physical and mental universe,' and he stresses that the mental aspect, and not the physical, should be emphasized. He emphasizes this because he says that most Shobogenzo scholars emphasize the physical aspect rather than the mental, and so forget themselves in the process. Genjokoan then, for Yasutani, means 'the subjective and objective realms are nothing but the Buddha dharma itself;' or, alternatively, 'what is manifest is itself absolute reality.' Most of the other translators reported in zensite also try, with varying success, to say what the word Genjokoan means: 'Actualizing the Fundamental Point,' 'The Actualization of Enlightenment,' 'Manifesting Suchness,' 'Manifesting Absolute Reality,' 'The Realized Law of the Universe,' and 'The Issue at Hand.' These attempts give examples of the problems that I say exist with the translations that I have referred to: *the translators are trying to find the exact English equivalent for the Japanese word 'Genjokoan.'* They believe that what concerned Dogen, when he was writing, can be precisely expressed in words, and are obviously not familiar with the above quotation from the Lankavatara. They seem equally unaware of the Zen master's injunction, "When you have the meaning you can throw away the words."

When Dogen wrote the Genjokoan, he was giving verbal directions to *that which has no form yet appears.* It appears as the subjective and objective realms. The emphasis though—Yasutani to the contrary—is not on the subjective or the objective realms. The emphasis is on '*that* which has no form yet appears.' I will prefer to use 'appears as' rather than 'appears to be' for the following reason.

You are no doubt familiar with heat waves that rise from the ground and look like a lake. Most people would say that the waves appear *to be* a lake. In this statement there is something—the waves—that appear to be something else—a lake. In other words the statement has a latent dualism. On the other hand, the expression 'the waves appear as a lake,' while containing a dualism, nevertheless expresses a unity. The expression, "dog no stone; stone no dog," is a useful metaphor.

Each of us has no form, yet we appear: we appear as a body, a personality, we appear as feelings and thoughts, sensations and ideas. The key word is 'appear.' We use the expression, "He appeared at the door," or "it appeared to be real but it was not," or "appearances deceive,' or "it appears that prices will fall." An ambiguity is present in the statement: something is and it is not. In the first, "he appeared at the door," the ambiguity is he is not there, yet he is there. In the second and third, "it appeared to be real but it was not," and "appearances deceive," the ambiguity is obvious. The final statement, "it appears that prices will fall," is saying that prices may fall and they may not fall. The ambiguity is very subtle in all the statements, but nevertheless it is real.

The word ambiguity is often used to denote vague or uncertain. However, in all that I have written I have used the term in a very special way. The Sufis use a word *unoambus* that means one/two. Each of us has no form yet we appear as a form. No form and form are two. Yet this is possible by virtue of "It," the One. Ambiguity, as I use it, means one/two. As we shall see, ambiguity runs through Dogen's Genjokoan.

The ambiguous phrase, "emptiness is form, form is emptiness," appears in the Prajnaparamita Hridya. In both cases the "is" is not the "is" of identity. For example, I can say, "That is a table." In this case I identify "that" with the word "table." I can either say "that" or "table" and I would say the same thing. But emptiness cannot be used instead of form. Emptiness is emptiness; form is form. It might be better to say, "emptiness appears as form; form appears as emptiness." 'It' has no form (emptiness) yet 'it' appears (as form).

Another, perhaps more obvious way of saying 'emptiness is form; form is emptiness' is to say, "Knowing is form; form is knowing." Knowing has no form yet when "I" see the road, the sky, and the trees, knowing (seeing) appears as the road, the sky, and the trees,

Zen master Tozan Ryokai wrote a verse that is called "The Real within the Apparent":

> A sleepy-eyed grandam
> Encounters herself in an old mirror.
> Clearly she sees a face,
> But it doesn't resemble her at all.
> Too bad, with a muddled head,
> She tries to recognize her reflection!

Before awakening we are all sleepy eyed grandams.

In the West the "subjective" has all but been ignored. 'Mind' and 'brain' mean more or less the same. The mind, at best, is considered to be an offshoot of the activity of the neurones of the brain. This gives an added difficulty to a Westerner studying Buddhism. Many of the principle Eastern thinkers see mind and body as one, although some are inclined to see mind as predominant and might even go so far as to say that the body is but a product of the mind. This way of seeing mind and body is clearly presented in the Lankavatara Sutra, much revered by Zen Buddhists. Bodhidharma is reputed to have taken the sutra to China It provides an understanding of the mind from a Zen Buddhist perspective.

We must bear in mind that while in the West we look upon the world as existent, and made of existent things, Buddhism is more inclined to look upon the world and mind as one and as an ongoing process. According to Buddhism, a basic characteristic of the world is impermanence. Dogen preferred the word *uji:* being/time. In other writings, I have used the expression, 'dynamic unity' rather than impermanence or uji. Dynamic unity is One yet appears to be two: mind and body.

To return, then to our original question, What does the word 'Genjokoan' mean? *"It has no form yet it appears."* A monk asked Ummon, "What is the dharmakaya?" "A brocade of a hundred thousand flowers."

COMMENTARY

1) Seeing that all things are the Buddha dharma, there is awakening, illusion, practice, life, death, buddhas, and sentient beings.

2) Seeing all things do not exist, there is no illusion, no realization, no buddhas, no sentient being, no birth and death.

3) Since the Buddha way is beyond form and emptiness, there are birth and death, delusion and enlightenment, sentient beings and buddhas.

We must bear in mind that the Genjokoan was written by an awakened man, Dogen. He wrote it in a letter to a student, telling how, after awakening, 'it' appears. Furthermore, as I mentioned earlier, after we awaken we perceive and live in the world in a new way; or rather, we live naturally. An awakened person lives *as* the world; a person who is not awakened lives *in* the world. We achieve or gain nothing when we awaken, in the same way that we achieve nothing when we wake up in the morning: we simply stop dreaming the dream of separation.

When we awaken, only the way we see things changes, not the things themselves. This is why I prefer to use the expression "Seeing all things…" All things are always the Buddha dharma. Because this is so, because all things are always the Buddha dharma, we can have the illusion that they are not the Buddha dharma, but are real in themselves. Because of this illusion, we have the illusion of practicing to awaken from the illusion, and, because there is the illusion of awakening, there is the illusion of buddhas and sentient beings.

The question then arises, what does Dogen mean when he says, *"Seeing that all things are buddha dharma..."* What does 'buddha dharma' mean?" I have chosen the subtitle, "'It' has no form, yet 'it' appears." 'It' is buddha dharma; it is not something. I use the word 'it' because our grammar demands that I do so. But even so, saying that 'it' is simply a grammatical device does not mean that it is nothing. The word 'dharma,' traditionally has a myriad different translations including 'the teaching of Buddha,' 'the universal law,' 'that which upholds.' I shall use the expression to mean, 'that which makes possible.'

Zen master Bassui, expresses *"Seeing that all things are buddha dharma..."* in this way:

> "The universe and yourself are of the same root, you and every single thing are a unity. The gurgle of the stream and the sigh of the wind are the voices of the master. The green of the pine, the white of the snow, these are the colours of the master, the very one who lifts the hands and moves the legs, sees and hears. The one who grasps this directly without recourse to reason or intellection can be said to have some degree of inner realization"

Awakening, illusion, practice, life, death, buddhas, and sentient beings are all in the nature of things. When we awaken, we do not awaken from the dream; we awaken to the dream. The dream is the dream that the dream is real.

The second verse reads, *Seeing all things do not exist, there is no illusion, no realization, no buddhas no sentient beings, no birth and death.* I am using the word 'exist' in its original sense. Etymologically, 'exist' is derived from two words: *ex* as in exit, or exodus, meaning 'outside of;' and *sister,* which is Latin for 'to stand.' 'Exist' therefore means to stand outside of, or separate from.

When we see things in a confused way, we see them as separate from ourselves, over there. In other words, we stand outside them. When we leave a room, we believe that the room remains unchanged from when we were in it. When we die, we believe that we 'leave the world,' and everything goes on as it was when we were alive, except we are no longer around to see it. We believe the sun will come up and the daily routine will be followed as it was when we were alive. As the saying goes, "We cannot take it with us." But what 'world' carries on after I die? What do I leave behind? My world, your world, the world of Bozo the cat? But I do not know, indeed I cannot know, your world or Bozo's world: I only know my own world, and I cannot leave that behind.

By the phrase 'my world' I mean the totality of my experience: past, present and potential. I do not simply mean what I am seeing with my eyes right at this moment. 'Seeing, or perceiving the world' is the result of a remarkably creative process involving our awareness, phenomena, our senses and language, as well as our memories, education and training.

To say that things do not exist, means that we no longer consider them to be separate from, or to stand outside of, being perceived; and so they are no longer considered to have a separate existence. Seeing is being, in the same way that emptiness is form: no seeing, no being. 'From the beginning, not a thing is,' as Hui Neng said. From the beginning, nothing stands outside. Therefore there is no world to leave behind, nor any person to leave it behind.

The third sentence reads, "*Since the Buddha way is beyond form and emptiness...*"

What does 'beyond' mean?

When you go to the cinema, you become lost in the film, enthralled by the love and hatred, by the conflicts and resolutions. When the film is over, all that is left is a white light shining on the screen. All that engaged you was simply a modification of the white light. You did not see the light during the entire film; the light was 'beyond' the film. The light had no form, but it appeared as the film, as the love and hatred, the conflicts and resolutions. 'It' has no form, yet it appears as birth and death, delusion and enlightenment, sentient beings and buddhas.

A cup has an outside and an inside. On the outside it has a pattern; on the inside is no pattern. Yet we drink tea then wash up the cup. Where then is there pattern or no pattern?

A painting by the Belgian painter Magritte illustrates the three verses very well.

The first of the above three verses represents form, the second, emptiness and the third beyond form and emptiness. In Magritte's painting, the form is the canvas, emptiness is the window, and you are the white light. Koans speak of these three in various ways: A monk asked Joshu, "What is Buddha?" "The Oak tree in the garden:" 'emptiness is form.' Emperor Wu asked a monk, "What is Buddha's light?" The monk walked away: form is 'emptiness'. A monk asked Nansen, "Is there a teaching that the Ancients did not teach? Nansen replied, "It is not mind, it is not Buddha, it is not things. It has no form yet it appears."

4) Yet, while this is true, and in spite of our wish that it were otherwise, flowers fall, and weeds spring up, even though we do not want them to.

This verse should really be included with the three above. It is only in the interests of clarity that I have separated it. It gives, in a concrete way, the truth to which the other three verses are pointing. Koans demand a demonstration, not an explanation. A demonstration does not necessarily involve a physical action; it can be what is called a capping phrase; a phrase like *flowers fall, and weeds spring up* expresses the truth in a non-explanatory way.

Nevertheless, in addition to demonstrating the import of the first three sentences, what Dogen is saying also brings out a very important point. In our culture we have "laws of the universe" that dictate what will happen; in Dogen's time it was karma that did the dictating. The second koan of the Mumonkan tells of a Zen master who was asked, "Does an awakened person fall under the law of causation or not?" and the master answered, "He does not." Because of this answer he lived as a fox for 500 lives. In order to be rescued from the life of a fox the master asked another master, "Is an awakened person subject to the law of causation or not?" The master answered, "He is one with the law of causation" - one with flowers falling and weeds flourishing.

A feature of Christianity is the presence of miracles. Jesus not only raised Lazarus from the dead, but was himself raised from the dead. He restored sight to the blind and hearing to the deaf. He even turned water into wine. This means that within the context of Christianity, an awakened person does not fall under the law of causation. For a person to be considered a saint, it has to be demonstrated that the would be saint had performed at least one miracle while alive. For a saint, 'flowers do not fall when it is time for them to fall, and weeds do not flourish when they are not bidden.' This same belief prevailed in Dogen's time. By paying homage to the gods, by making sacrifices and offering prayers and performing rituals, it was believed that the effects of karma could be diverted, and so one would not have to see flowers fall or weeds flourish.

Many people think that this is how it should be: if you are awakened then you are not subject to the vicissitudes of life. I remember a man expressing his disappointment on seeing a Zen teacher get up from the zazen mat in obvious pain from stiffness. The man felt that a teacher should be above such mundane concerns.

> " I thought I'd abandoned all-
> Even my body-
> And yet this snowy night is cold."

As Shakespeare had Hamlet say, "If it be now, 'tis not to come. If it be not to come, it will be now. If it be not now, yet it will come—the readiness is all."

5) Reaching out to experience the world is illusion; to allow the world to come to you is awakening. To awaken to the dream is buddhahood; to dream about awakening is to be an ordinary person.

The basic illusion that we have is the illusion of existence, which is the illusion of separation: the illusion that the reflections can be separated from the mirror. Similarly, to reach out to the world implies that the world is 'over there,' apart, separate from my seeing it. We are constantly reaching out: reaching out to be something, to know something, to do something, or to have something. This in turn is to see the world has having an independent reality. A reality towards which we reach.

"To allow the world to come to you is awakening." The operative word is 'allow.' To reach is intentional: one reaches in order to get, to find, to know, or to have something. To allow is to be receptive, actively open to the possibility. By way of example, suppose that you were asked to look after a group of children. You could control and organize their activities; or you could simply have no interest in what they did. Or, finally, you could allow them to play.

To allow is not a passive state. It is not 'acceptance' 'surrender,' or 'not doing anything.' To allow requires intense vigilance. Without vigilance we constantly slip back into reaching out. Allowing also requires that we do not interfere.

Practice is to allow. You can control the breath—slow the breath down, or lengthen the out-breath. Or, alternatively, you could sit and wait for something to happen. But, also, you could allow the breath to flow, while remaining vigilant. 'Allowing' is what the Chinese call *Wu Wei*. In his book *All and Everything,* Gurdjieff writes of the need for non-desires to predominate over desires, and Hubert Benoit writes of the "non-will to experience." These are different ways of talking about allowing. In his book *Zen in the Art of Archery,* the author Eugene Herrigel says that the master taught that one had to release the arrow but not intentionally; that is, one must 'allow' the arrow to be released.

To be able to allow, one must fully realize that nothing needs to be done, or, to use a Christian phrase, "Thy will be done." A monk went to Rinzai, made his bows, and was about to speak when Rinzai struck him. "Why do you strike me?" protested the monk, "I have not yet opened my mouth!" "What is the good of waiting until you have opened your mouth!" retorted Rinzai.

Buddhahood is to awaken to the dream, not from the dream,

> Thus shall you think of all this fleeting world:
> A star at dawn, a bubble in a stream;
> A flash of lightning in a summer cloud,
> A flickering lamp, a phantom and a dream.

To dream about awakening is to be an ordinary person. Hyakujo, when talking to Isan, said, "When you are awakened it is just like when you were not awakened." This will come as a surprise to most who dream of awakening as being elevated above the crowd, and being transformed into someone approximating a saint.

6) Moreover, some even awaken after awakening and others dream about the dream. An awakened person does not know he is awakened. Yet, even so, an awakened person continues as an awakened person.

"Moreover, some even awaken after awakening and others dream about the dream." In the book *Hakuin on Kensho*, Hakuin tells of four ways of being 'awakened after awakening.' The first awakening is the Great Mirror Awakening. This is awakening to the Dharmakaya, the 'vast emptiness and not a thing that can be called holy' that we read about in the first koan in the Hekiganroku. The emperor Wu asked Bodhidharma, "What are you teaching?" and Bodhidharma said, "Vast emptiness and not a thing that can be called holy."

The Dharmakaya is

> No-one
> Walks along this path
> This Autumn evening.

The second awakening is the awakening to equality. Bassui said, "The gurgle of the stream and the sigh of the wind are the voices of the master. The green of the pine, the white of the snow, these are the colour of the master, the very one who lifts the hands and moves the legs, sees and hears".

The third is awakening to differentiation. "Two monks roll up the blinds in an identical fashion." Zen master Hogen said, "One has it, the other does not." Everything is unique; there is no difference. Yasutani on one occasion said that even a cracked cup is perfect.

The fourth awakening is awakening to action. A monk asked Nansen, "Is there anything that the ancients did not teach?"

Nansen replied, "It is not mind, it is not body, it is not things."

A monk and his master were hoeing the garden. The master asked the monk, "What is it?" The monk stuck his hoe in the ground and stood up straight. The master said, "You have the essence, you do not have the function." The monk asked, "What is the function?" The master went on with his hoeing.

"*An awakened person does not know he is awakened.*" There was a teacher who would tell his students that they had come to awakening, even though the student had no knowledge of having done so. The teacher justified his action by quoting the above statement. However, the teacher quite missed the point.

An awakened person does not know he is awakened. God does not know he is God. This might be better said, "An awakened person is not conscious of being awakened." *Consciousness means knowing that something is the case.* It is the third of three levels of awareness. The first level is, for example, when I first go into a room I have a global, non-differentiated view of the room. The second level is when I focus on something in the room, say, the clock: 'I see the clock.' At the third level, the level of language I know the clock as a clock; I am conscious of it. I am conscious of seeing the "clock."

I could say this in a slightly different way.

I go into a room and at first I am simply aware-as the room, awareness and the room are undifferentiated. Then I am aware-of something in the room, let us say a clock. This

30

awareness would be aware-of awareness-as the clock. We are never simply aware-of the clock. We can only be aware-of-awareness-as it. Another way of saying this is that we are always in samadhi, not the samadhi that comes from practice, but which is our "True Nature."Awareness of awareness, or focused awareness, masks this truth.

The koan number 42 of the Mumonkan tells of this.

An actual example of the two forms of awareness is the following. It was given by a woman who said that she was standing at the edge of a low cliff overlooking the sea where birds were swooping in the sky when suddenly her mind switched gears. "I still saw the birds and everything around me but instead of standing looking at them, I was them and they were me. I was also the sea and the sound of the sea and the grass and the sky. Everything and I were the same, all one11" The expression, 'instead of standing looking at them, I was them' could be translated, using the terminology we have developed, as 'instead of standing, aware of awareness as them, I was just aware as them.' There was a diminution of 'awareness of' awareness as the birds, sea and grass, leaving simply 'awareness as' them.

We could say that consciousness is like two mirrors reflecting each other. One mirror is awareness-as, the other is awareness of.[4]

> A sleepy-eyed grandam
> Encounters herself in an old mirror.

---

[4] The metaphor of the mirror has two meanings.On the one hand it has the meaning of a substratum, in which case the emphasis of the metaphor is on the mirror, On the other it has the meaning of the illusory nature of phenomena, in which case the emphasis is on the reflections. The second of the two meanings is used here.

Simple awareness, on the other hand, is just one mirror: the mirror of One Mind

> Hearing, seeing, touching, and knowing are not one and one;
> Mountains and rivers are not to be seen in a mirror.

An awakened person does not know that he is awakened. "*Yet, even so, an awakened person continues as an awakened person.*" It is often believed that awakening means entering into a higher kind of consciousness, a Cosmic consciousness of some kind. Therefore, with awakening we leave behind the mundane consciousness. This is not so. An awakened person continues [but] as an awakened person.

7) Perceiving forms and sounds with a unified mind is intimate perception unlike reflections in a mirror or the moon reflected on water, when one side is light and the other darkness.

Consciousness—awareness reflected in the mirror of awareness—is always dualistic: when one side is light the other is darkness; if I am right then you are wrong. This dualistic state leads to a constant feeling of dissatisfaction, the feeling that Heidegger called *sorge*. Our true home is unity, wholeness. With consciousness we are always living the life of an alien, longing to return home, eternally wandering in search of that which we cannot lose. With a unified mind—free of reflection—perception is free of distance, free of separation. I am what I see; I am what I hear.

Where are you when a bird sings?

8) To know the Buddha Way is to know the self; to know the self is to forget the self; to forget the self is to be one with the ten thousand things. To be one with the ten thousand things means body and mind of oneself and others drop away. No trace of awakening remains, and traceless awakening goes on without end. At first, to seek the dharma is to be separate from the dharma. With authentic transmission true self is revealed.

Sometimes the first phrase of this verse, instead of being translated as, "To know the Buddha Way..." is translated as "To study the Buddha Way..." or, "To practice the Buddha Way...." However, Dogen says, "To know the Buddha Way is to know the self." If we translate that as, "To practice the Buddha way..." we can hardly go on to say, "is to practice the self." Furthermore, the word 'study,' "to study the Buddha Way" is too intellectual. One studies a subject with one's intellect; to know the Buddha Way is to be the Buddha Way.

"To know the self is to forget the self." Gurdjieff, a spiritual teacher who taught in Paris before the second world war, taught that we should remember ourselves. Both Gurdjieff and Dogen were teaching the same thing. Normally, to know the self is to know the self in the mirror of awareness. It is 'self-awareness' or 'self-consciousness.'

I sometimes ask in dokusan, "What are you?" and the student reflects on "I am." 'To reflect on' in this way is to stand outside of, to see from outside. This is why the student invariably replies, "the body" or "me" or something that can be pointed to.

However, to know the Buddha Way is to transcend the mirror of the mind, and in so doing the self of consciousness is forgotten; we now remember ourselves as we truly are. When we go beyond the mirror of the mind, *to see is to be*: To put this another way. "To forget the self, or to remember the self, is to be one with the ten thousand things;" Seeing is the ten thousand things. Then, body and mind drop away and, as Bassui says, "The gurgle of the stream and the sigh of the wind are the voices of the master. The green of the pine, the white of the snow, these are the colour of the master." No-one is left to say, "I am awakened," or "I am not awakened." As Hakuin would say, "True self is no self."

At first, to seek the dharma is to be separate from the dharma. With authentic transmission true self is revealed.

When we first begin to practice we are looking for awakening. We imagine it to be an experience that we can have; we see it something like a prize that we will receive for winning the race of practice. A prize, moreover, that others will admire and envy. But, with authentic teaching and practice the mists of ignorance dissolve, and the sun of true Self shines through.

> Monk: I have heard that men of old said, "It is void, it is clear, it shines of itself To shine of itself, what does that mean?"
> Joshu: It does not mean that something else shines.
> Monk: When it fails to shine what then?
> Joshu: You have betrayed yourself.

9) When sailing in a boat, and only looking just towards the river bank, one has the illusion that the shore is moving. But by fixing one's gaze just on the boat itself, one will see that the boat is moving. Similarly, viewing the ten thousand things with a confused mind we mistakenly believe that the mind and things are permanent. But, with the clarity of practice we will see that mind and things are empty.

Most readers, not having sailed on a boat, would be more comfortable hearing, "When sitting on a train and looking out of the window, you have the impression that the countryside is rushing by, with telegraph poles and wires manically dancing up and down. But if you fix your eyes on the inside of the carriage you will see that the train is moving." In much the same way when we see how fixed and stable the world seems to be, we have the impression that things and the mind are permanent and that they endure by themselves. But after we have truly practiced we see that the mind and things have no enduring quality, that indeed, everything is flowing.

10) Firewood turns to ash and cannot return to being firewood, but we should not believe that ash comes after and firewood before. Firewood is firewood and, having its past and future, is still independent of past and future. Ash is ash and has its own past and future. Just as firewood does not return to being firewood after it has become ash, we do not return to birth after death. This is the established rule of Buddhism and birth is known as the unborn. It is also the established rule of Buddhism that death does not become life. Thus death is known as no-death. Birth is now; death is now, just like winter and spring. We do not believe that winter becomes spring, nor spring summer.

This is one of the more difficult sections of the Genjokoan. In reading it we must remember that seeing is being. 'Seeing' and 'being' are verbs but they are also nouns: they are both actions and things. Hence things are *uji*, 'being time;' (things/action;) which means that things are dynamic, and not static, permanent things. Henri Bergson spoke of *durée*, and said that things do not simply change: things are change. We are used to the idea that things change because we know that they are constantly either growing or decaying, and also because science has told us that atoms are in fact dancing particles and waves. But Bergson was saying that there are no things that change: things are change

However, with *uji*, Dogen goes a step further than just saying that things are changing; he would agree with Bergson and say that things are change. Normally, we see change against a stable background. We see the telegraph poles dancing by because we see the carriage in which we are sitting as stationary. We see the carriage as moving when we see the countryside as stationary. We see the ash forming against the stable background of firewood. However, with uji, all is flowing: carriage and countryside, ash and firewood.

A common metaphor for time is a river. With a river the banks are stable and the river flows. Similarly, we believe that time flows against the background of eternity, which is stable. However, with uji, the banks also flow, or to put it another way, there is no eternity.

In the book, *Creating Consciousness*, I showed how consciousness evolved from knowing/being, through awareness-as, awareness-of, to consciousness. Earlier, I spoke of the progression through awareness-as, awareness-of, to consciousness. An American psychologist, Alison Gopnik, experimented with young children and came to the conclusion that a child's consciousness was quite different from that of an adult. She coined the phrase 'lantern consciousness' to describe the consciousness of young children, and 'spotlight consciousness' to describe the consciousness of adults. 'Lantern consciousness' corresponds to what I have called 'awareness-as'; 'spotlight consciousness' corresponds to 'awareness-of'.

Suppose that you want to find something in the basement but the basement is quite dark. You can either turn on the light or use a flashlight. By turning on the light, everything in the basement is illuminated equally at the same time; by using the flashlight you will light up one object at a time, the rest will remain in darkness. 'Lantern awareness' lights up the whole in an undifferentiated way; spotlight awareness focuses on one thing at a time.

Although adults use spotlight awareness, this does not mean that lantern awareness is no longer available to them. Spotlight awareness arises out of lantern awareness, much like waves emerge out of the sea. This means that I am aware-of (spotlight awareness) awareness-as (lantern awareness) the room.

The final step in the development of consciousness is 'naming.' We name that upon which spotlight awareness focuses. In this way what we are focused upon is fixed, much like passing a photograph through a chemical bath fixes the photograph. 'Fixing' gives it the appearance of permanence. 'Fixing' is made possible because a word remains unchanged and constant; it has no substance that can change. Words are not things; things are the result of words. The Mayans could not see the Spanish armada of ships that was bearing down on them because they had no word for 'ship.' Words are creations, and each time a person learns a new word, he or she recreates the word anew.

To return to Dogen's firewood: he does not see firewood as being 'over there,' separate from him. Firewood is 'uji,' or lantern awareness, that is subsequently focused upon by spotlight awareness and then called 'firewood.' What lantern awareness lights up is timeless; it is always now. Dogen sees the 'firewood now'; 'Firewood is firewood,' but it is also uji. Because the flow of uji is not a flow with reference to a stable point, uji does not flow in a direction.

A bus goes from Ottawa to Montreal. It moves through time, but as uji, it also flows, as do the seats in the bus and all else. As it moves through time it moves in a direction; the metaphor that we use for that is time's arrow. Once it has left Ottawa, it cannot return to Ottawa. All has changed; all is uji so all has changed, but this is not the change of going to Montreal and back, nor is it the change of atoms or subatomic particle. It is not a change from A to B; it is a change from A to A. A bus travelling to Ottawa is change *in* time; uji is change *as* time.

Just as ash does not return to being firewood, so we do not return after death. We die now, just as we are born now. There is not a succession of 'nows.' A succession of 'nows' would create the impression of a past and future, of a before and after. 'Dying now' means no death, just as being 'born now' means no birth. We know of death only through the death of others, as something happening in the world. In the same way, we know birth only through the birth of others. Being born now means that we cannot know birth except through the birth of others, just as dying now means that we can only know death through the death of others. Dying now means there is nothing to know, just as being born now means there is nothing to know. Dying is now; being born is now; with 'now' there is no inside or outside, known or unknown.

11) Coming to awakening is like the moon being reflected on water. The moon does not get wet nor is the water disturbed. Even though the moon's light spreads everywhere, it can be reflected in the shallowest of puddles. The great moon and the whole sky are reflected in the morning dew or a single drop of water. Awakening does not affect you any more than the moon disturbs the water. You cannot obstruct awakening, just as a puddle cannot obstruct the moonlight. The depth of the puddle is conditional on the height of the moon.

Coming to awakening is not an experience. An experience affects us in some way; it makes us feel something new or different. It adds to our knowledge, and affects the memory. Awakening is often accompanied by an experience that does affect us, but the experience is incidental. An example might help. You are flying to some important meeting. You are ready, the cases have been packed; the taxi that is to take you to the airport has arrived. You are just saying good-bye to your family, and you suddenly wonder whether you have the tickets. You look in your pockets...they aren't there. You look in the carry-on bag...they aren't there. You start searching all over the place. The taxi driver sounds his horn. You get frantic. You look under the chairs, between the cushions on the chairs. You run upstairs, downstairs and back upstairs again. You are searching everywhere. You come downstairs, and your wife asks, "Aren't these the tickets" YES! They were in the book that you are taking on the plane to read on the journey. You are overjoyed. You leap into the taxi shouting with joy, telling the driver about how you had found the tickets and what a relief it was.

The tickets were never lost; they were always in the book that you were going to carry on to the plane. In the same way they were not found. What is important is not the 'finding,' or the joy; what is important is that you get into the taxi. With awakening what is important is not the experience of joy, nor being liberated from the suffering induced by trying to live an impossible dilemma. Awakening is no change: t*he moon does not get wet nor is the water disturbed.*

Awakening does not affect you any more than the moon disturbs the water. A monk asked a brother monk who was awakened, "What is it like?" The brother monk replied, "Nothing special." *You cannot obstruct awakening, just as a puddle cannot obstruct the moonlight.* A master said, "Whatever you do is no good. Now, what are you going to do?"

Even though the moon's light spreads everywhere, it can be reflected in the shallowest of puddles. It does not matter whether one is dull or bright, successful or unsuccessful, rich or poor: awakening is awakening. Awakening can, however, be of different depths: the awakening of Buddha is likely to be much, much richer than the awakening of someone on a seven-day retreat in Canada; but the *quality* of the awakening is the same. It is like lighting a match in a cave or breaking through the roof of the cave and letting the sunlight stream through. The light of the match is feeble in comparison with sunlight, but the light is still light. The most profound demonstration of the koan "Every day mind is the way," is everyday mind. *The depth of the puddle is conditional on the height of the moon.*

12. When awakening is still mentally and physically incomplete, we believe that we have arrived. But with full awakening we feel something is missing. For example, if you sail to the middle of the ocean with no land in sight and look around in the four directions, the ocean looks circular with no distinguishing features. But the ocean is neither round nor square and its features are infinite. To fish, it is like a palace; to the gods it is like a jewelled necklace. But, as far as we are concerned, it is simply a vast circle of water. Though the material world and the transcendent world have a variety of features, you see and understand only what your eye of practice allows you to reach. So, if we want to know the way things really are, we should be aware that the oceans and mountains have an infinite number of aspects other than appearing square or round. We should also remember that there are other worlds in the four directions, not only out in space but also right here and now even in a drop of water.

Hakuin tells of his awakening in this way, "My pride soared up like a majestic mountain, my arrogance surged forward like the tide. Smugly I thought to myself: 'In the past two or three hundred years no one could have accomplished such a marvellous break-through as this.'"[5] He felt that he had arrived, and that his journey was complete. This is a familiar mistake that many of us make. Awakening has an incontro-

---

[5] Yampolsky, Philip (translator) (1971) *The Zen Master Hakuin*, Selected writings

(Columbia University Press: New York) P 118/9

vertible quality, a finality. Unity is unity. Yet we need to have awakening confirmed, simply because it is so easy to be confused by false awakenings. Not infrequently, I find myself assuring a student that he or she is not awakened, often over protestations of the student that I am mistaken. The Zen field is littered by self appointed 'senseis' and 'roshis' who have had either a samadhi experience, or a slight glimpse of their true nature, yet who are convinced that they have arrived and are equal to Buddha; they believe that they have the right to 'teach.'

Dogen said that there is no beginning to practice or end to awakening; there is no beginning to awakening or end to practice. Practice is a journey not an arrival. True awakening is an awakening to a more urgent need to go deeper. As Hakuin said, awakening is like the ocean, the further you go, the deeper it gets. Most who practice are fixated on the result, on the 'goal,' and in so doing become impatient with the process.

If you sail to the middle of the ocean with no land in sight and look around in the four directions, the ocean looks circular with no distinguishing features. Each of us knows only our own experience, and we have nothing with which to compare it. We can read of the experiences of others, but we interpret what we read, we make sense of it by relating it to our own experience. In doing so we not only distort others' experience, but we also make it our own. In other words we have not moved out of our own experience.

In the West, we believe that our understanding is only limited by the amount of experience that we have, whether that is university training or simple life experience. We feel the more experience we have, the greater our understanding will be. We do not have the notion of depth, level or richness of understanding. Since the seventeenth century, we have transferred our faith from the transcendent to reason and to its offspring, the technological.

Nowadays, we laud the spread and availability of information. We proclaim proudly that our age is the Information Age, believing that the more information that we have the wiser we will be. But, information must be integrated with experience before it is knowledge, and knowledge must be thoroughly digested and maturely integrated before it becomes understanding. Wisdom is the spiritual flower of which information is the roots, knowledge the stem, and understanding the leaves.

The idea that reason is the key to solving the mysteries of existence has been taken for granted for the last three hundred years. Consciousness is supreme. It is true that Freud's psychoanalysis questioned this belief, and Jung's collective unconscious added to our doubts, but with the advent of neuroscience the doubts have been laid to rest.

Knowing and awareness are now considered to be ghosts that no longer concern us because we cannot find an instrument that can register their influence.

13. A fish swims in the ocean, and regardless of how far it goes it does not come to the end of the water. A bird flies in the sky, and regardless of how far it flies it does not come to the end of the sky. However, the fish does not leave the water nor does the bird leave the sky. It is just that when they need to go far the sky and ocean are large; when they do not need to go far, the ocean and sky are small.

In this way, each fulfills itself to the utmost and uses its element to the fullest extent. If a bird should leave the sky it would instantly die and a fish would instantly die if it left the water. Water is life, the air is life; the fish is life, the bird is life. Many variations on this idea are possible: there is practice and awakening; there are people and activity.

A fish swims in the ocean; a bird flies in the sky; a human lives in the Way. Just as the ocean, even if it is the ocean of a fish-bowl, does not come to an end, and the sky has no limit, so the Way, too, is without limits. On the Way we fulfill ourselves and use the Way to our fullest extent. When our 'hunger and thirst for righteousness' is great, the Way is vast; when our 'hunger and thirst for righteousness is small' the Way is shallow. As Hakuin said: "Great doubt, great awakening; small doubt, small awakening. No doubt, no awakening." Water is life; the air is life; samadhi is life.

14. But if a bird tries to fly beyond the sky, or if a fish tries to swim beyond the ocean they will have no way, nor will there be any beyond. If we find the Way our daily activities manifest awakening; all our actions are the supreme reality. This Way is neither large nor small, self nor other, it does not exist from before, nor does it appear for the first time now, it is just thus.

A fish cannot swim out of the ocean, nor a bird fly out of the sky. We cannot fall out of awakening. Once we find the Way, as Layman P'ang would say,

> *What I do during the day is not unusual,*
> *I'm just naturally in harmony with them.*
> *Grasping nothing, discarding nothing,*
> *In every place there's no obstruction, no conflict.*
> *What is there that is exalted in that?*
> *From the hills and mountains the last speck of dust is cleared away*
> *My miraculous power and magical activity,*
> *Drawing water and carrying fire-wood.*

The Way has no limits; it is not yours or mine, and has no beginning or end, yet is not coming into being. It is not permanent or temporary, not eternal or bound by time.

15. Therefore, when practicing the Buddha Way, when realizing one aspect, one thoroughly penetrates that aspect; when engaged in one activity one is fully engaged in that activity. Now is the place; now the way unfolds. We cannot know the extent of what can be known because this knowing comes at the same time as awakening. Do not think that what you have seen into will inevitably be known consciously and will be recognized by your intellect. Although one awakens to the inconceivable all at once, it will not be experienced. How can it be?

A master said that to see through a speck of dust is to see through the whole universe.

In the sixties or seventies a magazine published by the ZCLA, called THE HAZY MOON OF ENLIGHTENMENT, published an article by Harada roshi, in which he speaks of "Proximate Zen."

"[In Proximate Zen] one is first given an old koan, and biting it sideways and up and down, looking at it and thinking about it many times in the wrong way, one falls into a tight spot. Then, unconsciously, one suddenly attains a bit of experience: "Oh, its probably this!" And so one passes that koan with a slight feeling of joy. After that, one by one, he passes fifty, a hundred or two hundred koans. In this way, a kind of proximate Zen is achieved..."

"Now the proximate Zen-master gives koans immediately to those who have not yet cultivated the root, and can't even believe in the principle of Buddha Nature or the law of causation. So it does not amount to anything and is only harmful, profiting no one..."

"....I can only sigh deeply when I see that nowadays there are too many proximate-Zen masters who are haphazardly teaching only proximate Zen or the Zen of samadhi of self-nature, regardless of the levels of the practitioners. Isn't there any master who wants to cultivate by practice the eye-power of the wisdom of the subtle observation?"

Proximate Zen is not Dogen's way of practice. One stays with the koan, ten, twenty, fifty years if necessary. Koan practice is not a way of learning about Zen. It is of no use to count the number of koans that you have 'passed.' It is like drilling for water: one does not dig a little hole here and another little hole there. One drills until the water gushes up.

But the kind of commitment that this calls for is not simply commitment to a way of practicing Zen: it is a way of life. Multiple tasking is now considered the way to get "the most out of life." Listening to music, texting, while studying is now the way to live. The attainment of a result is all that matters; the process is simply a means of attaining the result. This inevitably leads to living a life in order to be 'success-ful.' It also means that one is impatient, one does not enjoy the moment because the next moment might, must, or could be better.

The Zen way of life is commitment to the process. What I am doing now is all important. Patience is natural, as is satis-faction. One does not solve the problems of tomorrow because, as Jesus said, "Sufficient unto the day is the evil thereof." The only possibility in life is what is possible now. The Way unfolds now; knowing is now.

Knowing is the basis of consciousness and experience; we cannot know or experience knowing except in the mirror of knowing. It then is not knowing that we know, but a reflection. Awakening is to awaken beyond the mirror, beyond consciousness and the intellect. But this does not mean that awakening is, or can be, unconscious. Although we awaken as the inconceivable, it still remains inconceivable.

16. Zen master Pao-ch'e of Mount Ma-ku was fanning himself. A monk came and asked, "Wind, by its very nature, just keeps blowing, and there is nowhere it cannot reach. Why then do you need to use a fan? "The master replied, "You only know that the nature of wind is to keep blowing; you do not yet know the true meaning of 'there is nowhere it cannot reach.'" The monk the asked, "What is the true meaning of 'there is nowhere it does not reach'?" The master just fanned himself. The monk bowed deeply.

This is like authentic practice. Someone who says that because the wind just keeps blowing we do not need to use a fan, or even, even if we do not use [a fan] we can still feel the wind blowing, does not know ever-presence, and does not know ' there is nowhere it does not reach.' Because the very nature of wind is to keep blowing, the Buddha's Way reveals the Earth to be pure gold, and the Milky Way the sweetest of cream.

"From the beginning all beings are Buddha," why then do we need to practice? If we are already awakened, why do we spend years struggling to come to awakening? There are many so-called Zen teachers who say that indeed we do not need to struggle, or even need to practice. They do not know what is meant by, "From the beginning," nor "we are already awakened." It is because we are already awakened that we are impelled to practice, impelled to struggle. St. Augustine said, "If you had not already found Me you would not be seeking Me." "From the beginning" is not the beginning in time, but the beginning as origin; in our most profound depths we are Buddha, but at the surface we look outside. The monk's question was Dogen's life koan: if we are already awakened why do we need to struggle so hard to realize this?

Dogen taught Fukan Zazengi, "To practice the Way single-heartedly is, in itself, awakening." There is no gap between practice and awakening or zazen and daily life. I do not struggle and sweat to come to awakening. I do this to let go of the illusion that I am not awakened, the illusion that, to be fulfilled, I need something in experience. But I do not even know of this illusion until I practice. Someone asked Yasutani, "What is the difference between you and me?" Yasutani said, "No difference, except I know it."

But even so, "Before I practiced Zen, mountains were mountains, trees were trees. After I had practiced Zen, mountains were no longer mountains trees were no longer trees. But now, mountains are again mountains, trees are again trees."

Because we are already awakened the wonder of life never ceases.

Manufactured by Amazon.ca
Bolton, ON

20437169R00031